God Loves Me

CHERRI CAMPBELL

God Loves Me
Copyright © 2019 by Cherri Campbell
Victorious Faith Publishing

Bold type in the scripture quotations indicates the author's emphasis. Pronouns referring to the Father, Son, and Holy Spirit are capitalized while the name satan and related names are not capitalized. We choose not to acknowledge him, even to the point of violating grammatical rules.

Victorious Faith Publishing
info@victoriousfaith.co

ISBN: 978-1-951800-02-4 (Paperback)

Contents

Chapter One

─────◈─────

The Battle of the Mind

We've all experienced the battle of the mind when the enemy—the devil—comes to give us thoughts of defeat and failure, such as *"You're no good, you're not going to make it, there isn't going to be enough money this time, you're not going to get healed this time,"* etc.

If we don't do something about those thoughts, they will torment us and worry us day and night. We must learn that we have to cast those thoughts down, and we have to continue to speak God's promises instead—promises like: "God said He has good plans for me (Jeremiah 29:11), and He will fulfill His purpose for me (Psalm 138:8)!" "God said He supplies all of my needs (Philippians 4:19), and He watches over His word to perform it (Jeremiah 1:12)! I trust in Him, and He helps me

(Psalm 28:7)!'" One of my favorite promises is Hebrews 13:5 in the Amplified Bible (AMPC):

> *"for He [God] Himself has said, I will not in any way fail you nor give you up nor leave you without support. [I will] not, [I will] not, [I will] not in any degree leave you helpless nor forsake nor let [you] down (relax My hold on you)! [Assuredly not!]"* (brackets and parentheses are from the AMPC)

One time I was in one of those battles, and it was a moment by moment battle. I would speak God's promises, and the pressure would be relieved for a few minutes. But then the thoughts of worry would come again, and I'd have to say it again and believe it again.

Then the Lord began ministering to me once more about His love, reminding me *"Cherri, I love you!"*

Sometimes we can feel like God loves others, but maybe He doesn't love me very much, or He cares more about other people's needs than mine. But He spoke in my heart (not audibly), *"Cherri, I don't just love everybody else—I love you, and I want your needs met!"* He was reminding me of His love and care for me and that it isn't just for everybody else—it's for me!

We need to know that because 1 John 4:18 (KJV) says,

> *"There is no fear in love; but perfect love casteth out fear: because fear hath torment. He that feareth is not made perfect in love."*

There is no fear in love, and fear produces doubt. Fear is the source of doubt. Doubt is fearing that maybe it won't work, maybe God won't come through, maybe we won't get the money, maybe we won't get the healing, maybe it won't happen. That's fear because doubt is produced by and rooted in fear.

All doubt, worry, and anxiety are fear-based. So what is the cure for fear? Love. Specifically, it's knowing God's love for us. *"Perfect love casts out fear."*

God told us not to fear and why we shouldn't be afraid. Isaiah 41:10 says,

> *"So do not fear, **for I am with you**; do not be dismayed, **for I am your God. I will strengthen you and help you**; I will uphold you with my righteous right hand."*

God told us not to fear because He is with us and He will help us!

Anytime we are worried, anxious, wondering, or doubting, then we are in fear, and we are not perfected in love—a revelation of God's love for us. So if we would go back to the love foundation and build our faith in God's love for us, it will drive out fear, worry, and doubt.

Kinds of Love

How do we do that? First of all, we must understand what love is.

The lowest form of love is identified in the Greek language by the word "*eros*[1]" (this word is not used in the Bible). It is merely physical—it is physical affection based on feelings, especially sexual desire or passion. "This love is erotic [the word "*erotic*" comes from the Greek word "*eros*"]. *Eros* is a love of passion—an overmastering passion that seizes and absorbs itself into the mind. It is a love that is an emotional involvement based on body chemistry. The foundation of this type of love is some characteristic in the other person which pleases you. If the characteristic would cease to exist, the reason for the love would be gone, the result being, 'I don't love you anymore.' The basic idea of this love is self-satisfaction."[1] Because feelings are changeable—sometimes we say fickle—people fall in love and they fall out of love. That's the physical, *eros* kind of love.

There are three Koine Greek words translated "love" in the New Testament (the New Testament was written in Koine Greek)—*storge*, *phileo*, and *agape*. *Storge*[2] is compounded with *phileo* meaning "the mutual love of parents and children, and wives and husbands; cherishing one's kindred; loving affection; loving tenderly. It is chiefly the reciprocal tenderness of parents and children."[2]

Phileo[3] is often understood as "brotherly love." It means "to treat affectionately or kindly; to welcome, befriend; to show signs of love, to kiss; to be fond of doing [like 'I love to sing']."[3] Kenneth Wuest says, "It is a love that is called out of one's heart as a response to the pleasure one takes in a person or object."[4] *Phileo* "is a love that responds to kindness, appreciation, or love. It involves giving as well as receiving; but when it is greatly strained, it can collapse in a crisis."[1]

The greatest kind of love we see in the Koine Greek is the word "*agape*."[5] *Agape* is "called out of one's heart by the preciousness of the object loved. It is a love of esteem, of evaluation. It has the idea of prizing."[4] "It delights in giving. This love keeps on loving even when the loved one is unresponsive, unkind, unlovable, and unworthy. It is unconditional love. *Agape* desires only the good of the one loved. It is a consuming passion for the well-being of others."[1]

Agape is the God kind of love, and it is covenant love, and because it is covenantal—based on covenant—it never changes. It's not based on feelings. It's based on commitment. It is activated by choice and is a direction of the will. Because it is a choice not based on feelings, then no matter how you feel—if your feelings go up or your feelings go down—your commitment stays the same. It is covenantal commitment. It is demonstrated by action. It is unselfish. It is sacrificial. This is the kind of love that we need to grow in, and this is the kind of love that God has for us.

❦

Chapter Two

❦

Evidences of God's Love

W e've all heard "God loves you." **Many Christians superficially know that God loves them, but they don't have a true and deep sense and awareness of His love.** So how can we get a greater understanding and awareness that God loves us? Let's look at several evidences of His love.

God's Purpose for Man

For one thing, we know God loves us because of the reason why God made mankind—God's original purpose for mankind.

What do Christians usually say when you ask, "Why did God make man?" Many people say He made us to worship Him and/or to serve Him. But before God made mankind, God had angels. What do the angels do? They worship and serve Him, and the Bible says there are "thousands upon thousands, and ten thousand times ten thousand" (Revelation 5:11), and "innumerable hosts of angels" (Hebrews 12:22—ASV). God was already surrounded by myriads of angels, so why would He create mankind to do the same thing angels do? He didn't need any more creatures to worship and serve Him (not that we don't worship and serve Him—we do because we love Him, but it's not our primary purpose).

Our primary purpose for being created is because God *is* Love, and love (God) is never satisfied until it is expressed and shared! Love—the God-kind of love—is sharing deep affection and covenantal commitment between two people. It's both given and received. So God was not satisfied until He had someone to share His love with!

Genesis 1:26 (KJV) says,

"And God said, Let us make man in our image, after our likeness…"

First John 4:8 and 16 say,

"God is love."

We are created in the image of God, and God is love, so let's change the word "God" to "love"—

we are created in the image of love! We were made by Love Himself for love! That's our purpose![6]

The angels do not have the same capacity to love. They have their own capacity for emotions such as rejoicing over sinners when they get saved. But they don't have the same depth of capacity to love because they are not created in the image of God.

The animals also are not made in His image, and they're not made for love. Did you ever see a cow as it was eating grass, or a horse, or a dog, or a cat say, "I'm going to kill myself because nobody loves me"? But people do because love is a basic need of people.

We were made by Love Himself—the One who is Love—for love. Without love, some people don't want to live. Some people would rather die if they feel that no one loves them, and many times that's why they commit suicide. Why? Because love is a basic need of every human being.

Only mankind has the potential to love like God loves because we are made in His image! We have as much capacity in us—in our spirit being— as God has in Him with both the need and desire to give and receive love. God loves to love and to be loved, and it is our highest purpose—to be like Him.

God created mankind to have someone to love and to have friendship and fellowship with. That's why He walked with Adam in the cool of the day, that's why He called Abram His friend, that's why He talked to Moses face to face, and that's why He called David "a man after His own heart." And He wants to talk to you too! He wants *you* to walk with Him. He wants to call *you* His friend and call *you* the man or woman after His own heart just like He has throughout history with Adam, Abram, Moses, and David. He wants you to be His intimate friend every moment of every day!

God Made the Earth for Man

How else do we know that God loves us?

Look at what He made for us. God made the earth and the stars for mankind! Did you know that He did not make mankind for the earth? That's humanistic thinking, both modern and ancient humanistic thinking—save the trees, save the fish, etc. as if we live to serve nature. It's okay for you to preserve nature, but we were not made for the trees and fish. The trees and fish were made for us. God created the animals for us, and He said in Genesis 9:3,

"Everything that lives and moves will be food for you. Just as I gave you the green plants, I now give you everything."

They are here for us. We do not serve them, but we rule over them. Genesis 1:28 says,

"God blessed them and said to them, 'Be fruitful and increase in number; fill the earth and subdue it. Rule over the fish of the sea and the birds of the air and over every living creature that moves on the ground.'"

Psalm 8:6–8 say the same thing:

[6] "You made him to have dominion over the works of Your hands; You have put all things under his feet: [7] All sheep and oxen, yes, and the beasts of the field, [8] The birds of the air, and the fish of the sea, and whatever passes along the paths of the seas."

The earth was made for mankind, not mankind for the earth. Genesis 2:8–16 say that God planted a garden in the east called Eden, and in it were all kinds of trees, including the tree of life, a great river, and gold—which God said was very good! Psalm 115:16 says,

"The highest heavens belong to the Lord, but the earth he has given to man."

In other words, God put Adam in the garden and said, "This is for you—the gold is for you, the tree of life is for you, the river is for you. Everything is for you! The earth is for you!"

The reason all the stars and planets are here is so the earth could be here. The reason the earth is here is so that we could be here. He made it for us! That's why there are a sun and moon, and that's why every star twinkles. It's God heartily saying, "I love you, I love you, I love you!"

When you see the beautiful mountains, God is saying, "I put them there for you. I knew you'd like them." Every flower, every bird, the beautiful deer and elk, every ocean, every lake, every river and waterfall is God saying, "I love you! I made this for you! I knew you'd like it." Why? Because we are *"the apple of His eye"* (Zechariah 2:8)! In everything beautiful that you see, the Lord says, "I made it for you because I love you!" So, every day when you look at them, remember, "God loves me!"

He Delights In Us

The Bible also says God delights in us. Look at Isaiah 62:4–5 in the Amplified Bible (AMPC):

*⁴ **You** [Judah] shall no more be termed Forsaken, nor shall your land be called Desolate any more. But you **shall be called** Hephzibah [**My delight is in her**], and your land be called Beulah [married]; **for the Lord delights in you**, and your land shall be married [owned and protected by the Lord]. ⁵ For as a young man marries a virgin [O Jerusalem], so shall your sons marry you; and as the bridegroom rejoices over the bride, so shall your God rejoice over you.* (brackets are from the AMPC)

(Note: When you read promises in the Old Testament that speak to Judah, Israel, Jerusalem, Ephraim, etc., you can also receive them for yourself if you are born again[7] because in the New Testament, we are grafted into Israel [Romans 11:17–26; Ephesians 2:12–19]. So any promise that's for Israel is for us! You can put your name in it!)

Now put your name in for Judah:

"You, [Cherri, Stephen, Debbie]…*shall be called…'My delight is in* [her/him]*' …for the Lord delights in you!"*

Verse 5 talks about the bridegroom rejoicing over the bride, and in the New Testament, it says we are the Bride of Christ (2 Corinthians 11:2; Ephesians 5:25–27; Revelation 19:7–9; Revelation 21:2,9–11). So as a bridegroom is rejoicing over his bride, **Jesus is rejoicing over you**!

Now look at Zephaniah 3:17:

"The LORD your God is with you, he is mighty to save. **He will take great delight in you**, *he will quiet you with his love, he will rejoice over you with singing."*

The English Standard Version (ESV) says,

"The LORD your God is in your midst, a mighty one who will save; he will rejoice over you with gladness; he will quiet you by his love; he will exult over you with loud singing."

God's Word translation (GWN) says,

"The LORD your God is with you. He is a hero who saves you. He happily rejoices over you, renews you with his love, and celebrates over you with shouts of joy."

The Moffatt translation (Mof) says,

"The Eternal your God is in your midst, a warrior to the rescue; he thrills with joy over you, renews his love, exults with a festal song:"

And the New Jerusalem Bible (NJB) says,

> *"Yahweh your God is there with you, the warrior-Savior. He will rejoice over you with happy song, he will renew you by his love, he will dance with shouts of joy for you."*

Can you imagine God dancing with shouts of joy for you? Can you imagine God singing a happy song, thrilling with joy, and happily rejoicing over you? Can you imagine God celebrating and dancing over you with shouts of joy and a festal song? Think about it! God is dancing, singing, shouting, and rejoicing! Why? Because of you! O hallelujah!

Have you ever heard a secular love song with a person's name in it? They're singing about a girl, and they're saying her name, as in "Tammy, Tammy, Tammy's my love...."[8] Well, just think about God putting your name in His song: "Oh Mary, Mary, my love, I love you!" or "Mark, my son, I love you!" God is singing over you, rejoicing over you, and shouting and dancing over you, and His song has your name in it! Praise the Lord!

He Chose Us

We also know from scripture that God chose us. John 15:16 says,

> *"You did not choose me, but I chose you...."*

Ephesians 1:4–5 say,

> *"For he chose us in him before the creation of the world to be holy and blameless in his sight. In love ⁵ he predestined us for adoption to sonship through Jesus Christ...."*

Ephesians 1:11 says,

> *"In him we were also chosen...."*

Colossians 3:12 says,

> *"Therefore, as God's chosen people, holy and dearly loved...."*

First Thessalonians 1:4 (NLT) says,

> *"We know, dear brothers and sisters, that God loves you and has chosen you to be his own people."*

And 1 Peter 2:9 says,

> *"But you are a chosen people...."*

We know He loves us because He chose us. He chose us because He loves us!

We Are Precious to Him

We also know that we are precious to Him. Isaiah 43:4 says,

> *"Since you are precious and honored in my sight, and because I love you…."*

We Are Beautiful to Him

Isaiah 62:3 (AMPC) says we are beautiful to him:

> *"You shall also be [so beautiful and prosperous as to be thought of as] a crown of glory and honor in the hand of the Lord, and a royal diadem [**exceedingly beautiful**] in the hand of your God"* (brackets are from the AMPC).

You are exceedingly beautiful!

Zechariah 9:16–17 say:

> *"The LORD their God will save his people on that day as a shepherd saves his flock. They will sparkle in his land like jewels in a crown. [17] How attractive and beautiful they will be!"*

Then look at Song of Solomon. The whole book is a picture of God's love for us. Song of Solomon 1:15 says,

> *"How beautiful you are, my darling! Oh, how beautiful!"*

That's how the Lord sees us. We are beautiful to Him!

We Are Valuable to Him

And we are valuable to Him. Matthew 6:26 says,

> *"Look at the birds of the air; they do not sow or reap or store away in barns, and yet your heavenly Father feeds them. Are you not much more valuable than they?"*

Matthew 10:29–31 say:

> *"Are not two sparrows sold for a penny? Yet not one of them will fall to the ground outside your Father's care. [30] And even the very hairs of your head are all numbered. [31] So don't be afraid; you are worth more than many sparrows."*

Have you ever tried counting your hairs? No, but God does! That's how much He cares and loves you!

Matthew 13:45–46 say,

"Again, the kingdom of heaven is like a merchant looking for fine pearls. [46] *When he found one of great value* [great price—KJV]*, he went away and sold everything he had and bought it."*

This parable is about you. *You* are the pearl that God found, and He sold Jesus, gave Jesus' life, so that He could buy you—so He could redeem you back from the enemy's hand! *You* are the pearl of great value and great price that He found!

He Paid A Great Price For Us!

Do you know how else you know He loves you? He paid a great price for you!

Psalm 49:7–8 say,

"No one can redeem the life of another or give to God a ransom for them— [8] *the ransom for a life is costly, no payment is ever enough."*

No natural payment is ever enough, but there was one thing in all the universe that was able to pay the price, and it was the blood of the spotless Lamb of God, Jesus! John 3:16 (KJV) says,

> *"For God so loved the world, that he gave his only begotten Son, that whosoever believeth in him should not perish, but have everlasting life."*

God thinks you are worth saving. You're worth it! Jesus said you're worth it all—the whipping post, the crown of thorns, suffering the nails in His hands and feet, dying on the cross—He says you're worth it! You're worth it, praise the Lord! God thinks you're worth saving!

He first created you in His image, but He lost you to sin, and so He paid for you again by His blood to get you back. That's what redemption means—to buy back again. We are twice His, hallelujah!

First Peter 1:18–19 say:

> *"For you know that it was not with perishable things such as silver or gold that you were redeemed from the empty way of life handed down to you from your ancestors, [19] but with*

the precious blood of Christ, a lamb without blemish or defect."

We were bought with the precious blood of Jesus. Salvation was not cheap. The price was very high—it cost God the blood of His only Son! It cost Jesus death and the terrible suffering of crucifixion, being made sin for us (2 Corinthians 5:21), carrying every disease (Matthew 8:17) and the curse of sin and death (Galatians 3:13), and even enduring the horror of Hell for us (Acts 2:27,31—KJV; Romans 10:7).

Your worth is found in the price paid for you, and that cannot be measured because the blood of Jesus is more valuable than anything in all creation!

The Great Exchange

Isaiah 43:4 once again says,

"Since you are precious and honored in my sight, and because I love you, I will give [Jesus] ***in exchange for you...in exchange for your life."***

Jesus made the great exchange!

* He was accused, convicted, and condemned in order to justify, acquit, vindicate, and pardon

you (Isaiah 53:8; Mark 14:55–64; Isaiah 54:17; Isaiah 55:7; Romans 3:24; Romans 5:9).

* He was made to be sin so that you could be made the righteousness of God in Him (Isaiah 53:5–12; 2 Corinthians 5:21).

* He was shamed and disgraced so that you could be given glory and honor (Hebrews 12:2; 2 Corinthians 3:18; Romans 2:10).

* He was rejected so you could be accepted (Isaiah 53:3; Romans 15:7; Ephesians 1:6 KJV).

* He was forsaken so that you will never be forsaken or abandoned (Psalm 22:1; Matthew 26:56; Matthew 27:46; Deuteronomy 31:6,8; Hebrews 13:5)

* He bore the chastisement of your peace and gave you His peace (Isaiah 53:5; John 14:27; John 16:33; Ephesians 2:14)

* He bore your griefs and sorrows and gave you His joy (Psalm 30:11; Isaiah 53:3–4; Isaiah 61:3; Jeremiah 31:13; John 15:11; John 17:13)

* He was oppressed and afflicted to make you free (Isaiah 53:7; Luke 4:18; John 8:36; Galatians 5:1)

* He was separated from God so that you could be brought near to God (Matthew 27:46; Ephesians 2:13; Hebrews 10:19–22).

* He bore your sicknesses so that you could be healed (Isaiah 53:4; Matthew 8:17; 1 Peter 2:24).

* He was made poor so that you could be made rich (2 Corinthians 8:9).

* He died so you could live (Romans 6:4–5).

* He went to hell so that you could go into the presence of God in heaven and live there with Him forever (KJV Acts 2:27,31; Romans 10:7; John 14:3; 1 Thessalonians 4:16–17)!

He took your place and gave you His! He made the exchange for you! Praise God!

Your Worth Is His Worth

You're worth is also found in the One who purchased you and brought you into His family. If you were born into a very, very wealthy family, your worth would be found in the family that you are born into. How much is God worth? Your worth lies in His worth because when you are born again[7], you are born into His family. (If you're not born again[7] yet, then pray the prayer of salvation at the end of this book. Instantly, you will be saved and brought into His family!)

So how much is God worth? He owns the whole universe—the heavens and the earth and all that is in it (Psalm 89:11; Psalm 50:10–12; Haggai 2:7–8)! His worth is incalculable. Your net worth goes up just because you are His child, and He salvaged you, bought you, and brought you into His family! Now your worth is His worth!

He Loves Us as Much as He Loves Jesus

The Bible says He loves us as much as He loves Jesus! John 17:23 (NET) says,

> *"...you have loved them just as you have loved me."*

That's why He gave Jesus in exchange for us.

We can only try to imagine how much God loves Jesus, and He loves you the same because He gave Jesus in exchange for you! Praise the Lord!

His Love Is Incomprehensibly Great!

His love is incomparably and incomprehensibly great! Psalm 36:5 says,

"Your love, Lord, reaches to the heavens, your faithfulness to the skies."

His love reaches to the heavens! That cannot be measured. How far is it to the outer edge of the universe and beyond? That's how far His love reaches—farther than the outer limits of all creation.

John 15:13 (NKJV) says,

> *"Greater love has no one than this, than to lay down one's life for his friends."*

And Jesus did that. He fulfilled the greatest love of all by laying down His life for us.

First John 3:1 says,

> *"See what great love the Father has lavished on us, that we should be called children of God! And that is what we are!"*

I like the word *lavished*. He *lavished* His love on us calling us His children!

The Amplified Bible (AMPC) says,

> *"See what [an incredible] quality of love the Father has given (shown, bestowed on) us…."*

The word incredible also means "amazing and extraordinary," so you could say, "what amazing and extraordinary love the Father has given, shown, and bestowed on us that we should be called the children of God."

Ephesians 2:4–5 (AMPC) say:

"But God—so rich is He in His mercy! Because of and in order to satisfy the great and wonderful and intense love with which He loved us... ⁵ Even when we were dead (slain) by [our own] shortcomings and trespasses, He made us alive together in fellowship and in union with Christ; [He gave us the very life of Christ Himself, the same new life with which He quickened Him, for] it is by grace (His favor and mercy which you did not deserve) that you are saved (delivered from judgment and made partakers of Christ's salvation)."
(brackets and parentheses are from the AMPC)

Because of the great, wonderful, and intense love with which He loved us, in His grace, favor, and mercy He gave us the very life of Christ Himself! That was the expression of His great, wonderful, and intense love!

God Demonstrated His Love

How do we know God loves us? Love is action. Love cannot be inactive. When love sees the person that it loves, it wants to do something. Love has to be expressed. So God acted. God saw us in our need of being lost and in bondage to sin and satan, and so John 3:16 (KJV) says,

> *"For God so loved the world, that he gave his only begotten Son...."*

He was moved to action to give His Son for us because He loved us. Romans 5:8 says,

> *"But God demonstrates his own love for us in this: While we were still sinners, Christ died for us."*

Verse 10 says,

> *"For if, while we were God's enemies, we were reconciled to him through the death of his Son, how much more, having been reconciled, shall we be saved through his life!"*

While we were still God's enemy—we hadn't called on Him, and we didn't love Him—He died for us. If He loved us then, how much more can we live and walk in His love now when we're His children!

First John 4:9–10 say:

> [9] *"This is how God showed his love among us: He sent his one and only Son into the world that we might live through him. [10] This is love: not that we loved God, but that he loved us and sent his Son as an atoning sacrifice for our sins."*

He loved us, and He set us free so that we can live through Him. Revelation 1:5 says,

> *"To him who loves us and has freed us from our sins by his blood…"*

So, the birth of Jesus when He came into the world to be our Savior, and His death, said to the world, "I love you, I love you, I love you, world!" Hallelujah!

God Is a Good God and He Wants Good Things for You

How else do we know God loves us? The Bible says He is a good God, and He wants good things for us. Psalm 119:68 says,

"You are good, and what you do is good."

When Moses said to God *"show me your glory"* in Exodus 33:18, God answered him in verse 19:

*"I will cause all my **goodness** to pass in front of you"*

God's goodness is His manifested presence and glory. Excellent goodness is who God is!

Psalm 52:1 (KJV) says,

"...the goodness of God endureth continually."

Psalm 145:9 says,

*"The Lord is good to **all**; he has compassion on **all** he has made."*

Unbelievers will often say, "If God is a loving God, then why is there death, pain, violence, sickness, and hunger in the world?" Because there is sin in the world! Sin is the parent of death, and death is the parent of sickness, disease, pain, lack, hunger, strife, and violence. It's also called the curse of sin and death that came through Adam. Romans 5:12 (NKJV) says,

"Therefore, just as through one man sin entered the world, and death through sin, and thus death spread to all men, because all sinned --"

God is not the cause of the problem—sin is. But God sent His Son as the cure for the problem! And He made His cure available to everyone!

Christians also ask, "If God loves me, then why did this bad thing happen in my life? Why did my loved one get killed in a car accident or die of cancer? Why do I have these problems?" Religious traditions say that God has a purpose for it, but that is not true! No bad thing ever comes from God or is God's will! John 10:10 says,

"The thief comes only to steal and kill and destroy; I have come that they may have life, and have it to the full [more abundantly— KJV]."

God is not the thief—satan is. Satan comes to steal, kill, and destroy. Anything and everything that is stolen, killed, or destroyed was stolen, killed, or destroyed by satan, not God! We have to recognize who our enemy is, and it is satan. God is not the cause or the permitter of evil.

Jeremiah 29:11 says,

> *"For I know the plans I have for you,'* *declares the* LORD, **'plans to prosper you** **and not to harm you**, *plans to give you hope and a future.'"*

The Complete Jewish Bible (CJB) says,

> *"…plans for well-being, not for bad things…"*

The New Living Translation (NLT) says,

> *"…They are plans for good and not for disaster…"*

The New American Standard (NAS) says,

> *"…plans for welfare and not for calamity…"*

God's plans are **only** for good and not for bad!

Jesus said that He came to give life "more abundantly." The Greek word translated "more abundantly" in John 10:10 and translated "exceeding abundantly" in Ephesians 3:20

> *(KJV—"Now unto him that is able to do* **exceeding abundantly** *above all that we ask or think, according to the power that worketh in us,")*

means "superior, extraordinary, surpassing, super-abundant, uncommon, in a greater degree, beyond measure, far over and above, excessive."[2] That's the kind of life God wants you to have and that Jesus died for so you could have!

Third John 1:2 (KJV) says,

"Beloved, I wish above all things that thou mayest prosper and be in health, even as thy soul prospers."

Deuteronomy 8:7–10 say:

[7] *"For the Lord your God is bringing you into a good land—a land with brooks, streams, and deep springs gushing out into the valleys and hills;* [8] *a land with wheat and barley, vines and fig trees, pomegranates, olive oil and honey;* [9] *a land where bread will not be scarce and you will lack nothing; a land where the rocks are iron and you can dig copper out of the hills.* [10] *When you have eaten and are satisfied, praise the Lord your God for the good land he has given you."*

God wants good things for you!

He's the Ultimate Gift Giver— He Has Given Us Great Gifts!

How do we know God loves us? Because He has given us great gifts! He's the ultimate gift giver! God is good, and He's giving good gifts all the time. Psalm 31:19 says,

> *"How abundant are the good things that you have stored up for those who fear you, that you bestow in the sight of all, on those who take refuge in you."*

Psalm 68:19 (KJV) says,

> *"Blessed be the Lord, who daily loadeth us with benefits…"*

Psalm 103:2-5,11 say,

> *"² Praise the LORD, O my soul, and forget not all his benefits— ³ who forgives all your sins and heals all your diseases, ⁴ who redeems your life from the pit and crowns you with love and compassion, ⁵ who satisfies your desires with good things so that your youth is renewed like the eagle's. ¹¹ For as high as the heavens are above the earth, so great is his love for those who fear him;"*

Psalm 145:7–9 say,

> *"⁷ They celebrate your abundant goodness and joyfully sing of your righteousness. ⁸ The Lord is gracious and compassionate, slow to anger and rich in love. ⁹ The Lord is good to all; he has compassion on all he has made."*

James 1:17 says,

> *"Every good and perfect gift is from above, coming down from the Father…"*

He is continually pouring out gifts, and that's the root meaning of the word *grace*: *gifts*. Whenever you see the word *"grace"* in the New Testament, translate it "free gifts." Grace is also the charitable, benevolent heart of the giver that loves to give lavishly, and it is the grateful heart of the receiver.

His grace is His abundant gifts that He's lavishing on us all the time. *"By grace through faith"* means grace is the hand of God extended and open to you, giving you all that He has. His entire kingdom of heaven is yours—it's a free gift! That's grace. Grace is God's arm and open hand extended to you with His gifts. Faith is your arm (spiritually) that reaches up to take hold of what God gives you. God gives by grace, but we receive everything He gives by faith.

He extends His arm and open hand of grace—free gifts—to the whole world, but there are a lot of people who don't receive from Him because it's by faith that we receive. Since faith is our arm that reaches out and takes hold of what He freely gives, therefore without faith, the gifts will be unopened and the promises will not be manifested.

Faith is what takes hold of God's gifts and receives them personally. The Greek word translated *"receive"* in the New Testament is the word *"lambano,"* and it means "to take with the hand, to lay hold of (anything in order to use it), to take to one's self, to make one's own, to claim, to procure for one's self, to seize, to take possession of, to appropriate to one's self."[10]

In the Greek, *"receive"* is not a passive or inactive word. It is an aggressive, assertive, and active word! Every day we need to say, "Lord, I believe I receive your gifts and your abundant goodness in my life!" And then take the promises (the whole Bible is full of promises) for what you need by faith and believe you receive them (believe you take them).

That's why Hebrews 4:16 says,

"Let us then approach God's throne of grace [free gifts] *with confidence, so that we may*

> *receive* [lay hold of and take to one's self]
> *mercy* [getting good things we don't
> deserve] *and find grace* [free gifts] *to help
> us in our time of need."* (brackets mine)

I love that scripture!

God has given us so many great gifts! We already mentioned the new birth and salvation, and He has given us sonship in His family.

He also gave us the Holy Spirit. Jesus said in John 14:16–17:

> *"And I will ask the Father, and he will give
> you another advocate to help you and be with
> you forever—*[17]*the Spirit of truth. The world
> cannot accept him, because it neither sees him
> nor knows him. But you know him, for he
> lives with you and will be in you."*

The Holy Spirit is given to you to anoint you, help you, teach you, guide you, intercede for you, comfort you, empower you, and give you revelation. The Holy Spirit is your Comforter, Helper, Counselor, and Teacher. When God gave you the Holy Spirit, He was saying to you, "I love you!"

God gave us all the gifts of the Holy Spirit. First Corinthians 12:7–11 list nine gifts or manifestations of the working and service of the Holy Spirit through believers: the word of wisdom, word of knowledge, faith, gifts of healings, working of miracles, prophecy, discerning of spirits, divers kinds of tongues, and interpretation of tongues. He gave us these special gifts because He loves us.

He also gave us the ministry gifts. Ephesians 4:11–12 say,

> *"So Christ himself* **gave** *the apostles, the prophets, the evangelists, the pastors and teachers, 12 to equip his people for works of service, so that the body of Christ may be built up."*

These ministers are a gift to the body of Christ and to the world because God loves us. He gave these to you to evangelize you, teach you, equip you, and train you to fulfill God's calling on your life to receive what He has for you and to do the work He called you to do. These ministers are God's gift to you saying, "I love you!"

He gave us His Word, the Bible, as it says in 2 Peter 1:4,

> *"Through these he has given us his very great and precious promises, so that through them you may participate in the divine nature…"*

What does the Word of God do for us? The Word is a lamp and light for our path (Psalm 119:105). The Word is our spiritual bread, milk, and meat (Matthew 4:4; Hebrews 5:11–14; 1 Peter 2:2). The Word is life, health, and medicine for your body (Proverbs 4:20–22). The Word is truth that makes you free (John 8:32; John 17:17). The Word is the wisdom, answer, and solution for every problem and situation in life (Proverbs 4:4–13). The Word is everything you need (2 Peter 1:3)! And He gave you His Word—His very great and precious promises—because He loves you!

God gives us life and breath as Paul preached when he was in Athens in Acts 17:25,

> *"...he himself gives everyone life and breath and everything else,"*

and in verse 28,

> *"For in him we live and move and have our being."*

So every time your heart beats, God is saying, "I love you, I love you, I love you! I give you this heartbeat, I give you this breath because I love you!" Hallelujah! Praise the Lord!

He meets all of our needs, as He said in Philippians 4:19 (KJV),

"But my God shall supply all your need according to his riches in glory by Christ Jesus."

That means your home, your vehicle, your clothes, your food, your phone—His continuous daily provision—everything you have is God saying, "I love you!"

Second Peter 1:3 (NKJV) says,

*"His divine power has given to us all things that pertain to **life** and **godliness**, through the knowledge of Him."*

"Life" refers to your physical needs, and *"godliness"* refers to your spiritual needs. He gives you everything you need for both your physical and your spiritual needs through your knowledge of Him. So there again, it comes by revelation of the Word of God and receiving it by faith.

He Wants to Satisfy Our Desires

God loves you so much that He wants to satisfy your desires! Many Christians think that God will meet your needs, but He won't give you all of your desires. But that would be a stingy God. If you are a parent and you love your children, and if your children want a toy, don't you want to give it to them if you have the ability? If they want something good, don't you want to give it to them if you have the ability? God does, and He has given us many promises that He will satisfy our desires!

> Psalm 21:2 *"You have granted him his heart's* **desire** *and have not withheld the request of his lips."*

> Psalm 37:4 (NAS) *"Delight yourself in the LORD; And He will give you the* **desires** *of your heart."*

> Psalm 103:2–5 *"Praise the LORD, O my soul, and forget not all his benefits—³ who forgives all your sins and heals all your diseases, ⁴ who redeems your life from the pit and crowns you with love and compassion, ⁵ who satisfies your* **desires** *with good things so that your youth is renewed like the eagle's."*

> Psalm 145:16 *"You open your hand and satisfy the* **desires** *of every living thing."*

> Psalm 145:19 *"He fulfills the* **desires** *of those who fear him"*

> Proverbs 10:24 *"…what the righteous* **desire** *will be granted."*

He wants to satisfy you and grant your desires! God doesn't say "No" to any good thing!

Matthew 7:7 says,

*"Ask and it **will be** given to you; seek and you will find; knock and the door will be opened to you."*

John 15:7 says,

*"If you remain in me and my words remain in you, ask whatever you wish, and it **will be** done for you."*

That means that when you stay connected to Him and to His Word, then you will have righteous desires and ask for good things that He is eager to give. That is the meaning also of Psalm 37:4 (above) because when you are delighting in Him, you are delighting to do His will. Then His will produces righteous and good desires in your heart that He is eager and ready to give!

Both of these verses say *"**will be**."* They *will be* given to you! He delights in giving you your heart's desires!

Second Corinthians 1:20 says,

"For no matter how many promises God has made, they are 'Yes' in Christ. And so through him the 'Amen' is spoken by us to the glory of God."

His promises for good things are always "yes" to us!

I know many Christians ask, "Then why don't I have them?" Because our part is to learn from His Word *how* to receive them! It comes through the knowledge of His Word and His ways, as it says in 2 Peter 1:3.

Everything He Has, He Gives!

He gives us everything! When we are born again[7], He gives us His kingdom. Luke 12:32 says,

"...your Father has been pleased to give you the kingdom."

Romans 8:32 says,

"He who did not spare his own Son, but gave him up for us all—how will he not also, along with him, graciously [or freely] *give us **all** things?"*

Because He gave you Jesus, He will not withhold anything! So if He gave you Jesus, He will heal your body. If He gave you Jesus, He will pay your bills. If He gave you Jesus, He will give you a home, a car, a job, fix your marriage, and restore your relationship with your children or whatever else you need.

Do you remember what the father said to the older son in the parable of the two sons (what is normally called the parable of the prodigal son)? Luke 15:31 says,

> *"'My son,' the father said, 'you are always with me, and everything I have is yours!'"*

Just like the older son, many Christians today often forget that everything the Father has is theirs now, and they complain about what they don't have. Just like the older son, they live without enjoying the pleasures, benefits, and provisions that God has already made available, and they ask God, "Why don't you give me a car? Why don't you heal my diabetes? Why don't you… why don't you…?" And the Father is looking at you saying, "Son/daughter, everything I have is yours! It's a free gift! I give you the kingdom! Come boldly and lay hold of it by faith! It's yours!" And that's a key. We have to receive it by faith—laying hold of it, claiming it, and possessing it (the Greek definition of "receive"[10]).

If God were ever going to hold anything back from us, it would have been His Son, but He didn't even withhold His Son. And with His Son, He freely gives us **all** things (Romans 8:32)!

He Never Forgets Us

How else do you know God loves you? He never, never forgets you—never for a second, not even a microsecond! He is always thinking of you!

Isaiah 49:15–16 in the Amplified Bible (AMPC) say:

> *"[And the Lord answered] Can a woman forget her nursing child, that she should not have compassion on the son of her womb? Yes, they may forget, yet I **will not forget you**. [16] Behold, I have indelibly imprinted (tattooed a picture of) you on the palm of each of My hands; [O Zion] your walls are continually before Me."* (parentheses and brackets are from the AMPC)

Do you keep a picture of a loved one with you, maybe in your wallet or on your desk or dresser, to remember them and think of them? God has your picture engraved and tattooed on the palms of His hands! Have you ever seen anybody tattoo the picture of their loved one on their body?

Maybe their name, but their picture? Probably not. But God does! God tattoos your picture on the palms of His hands, and all He has to do is look at His hand and say, "Oh Mary/John, my beloved, my daughter/my son, I love you so much!" And you are continually before Him all the time, 24/7! Every microsecond! Hallelujah! Praise the Lord! He never forgets us! He is always thinking of us!

He Is Interceding for You

Jesus is still giving today, and He's still serving the Church today.

The four Gospels—Matthew, Mark, Luke, and John—are the record of Jesus' ministry on earth. The book of Hebrews is the record of Jesus' ministry in heaven now, and it says He is our high priest (Hebrews 2:17; 3:1; 4:14–15; 6:20), and He is our intercessor. Hebrews 7:25 says,

> *"he always lives to intercede for them* [those who come to God through Him].*"*

Jesus is praying for you every moment! If you need a prayer partner, if you need someone to pray for you and intercede for you, you have one! You have Jesus!

Romans 8:27 says the Holy Spirit is also interceding for us:

"And he who searches our hearts knows the mind of the Spirit, because the Spirit intercedes for God's people in accordance with the will of God."

So Jesus is interceding for you *and* the Holy Spirit is interceding for you. You are never without prayer and intercession!

❦

Chapter Three

❦

His Love Is Everlasting

T hank God, His love is everlasting! It will never fail! Jeremiah 31:3 says,

> *"I have loved you with an **everlasting** love; I have drawn you with unfailing kindness."*

Not only is it everlasting, but Ephesians 2:4–7 say it's for the ages to come:

> *[4] "**But because of his great love for us**, God, who is rich in mercy, [5] **made us alive with Christ** even when we were dead in transgressions—it is by grace you have been saved. [6] And God **raised us up with Christ and seated us with him** in the heavenly realms in Christ Jesus, [7] **in order that in the coming ages he might***

show the incomparable riches of his grace, *expressed in his kindness to us in Christ Jesus."*

Because He loves you, He raised you up with Him and seated you with Him in the heavenly realms. That is your spiritual position and seat when you are born again[7]. Verse 7 says,

> *"in order that in the coming ages* [Greek text—eons] *he might show the incomparable riches of his grace, expressed in his kindness to us in Christ Jesus."*

The Amplified Bible says,

> *"He did this that He might clearly demonstrate through the ages to come the immeasurable (limitless, surpassing) riches of His free grace (His unmerited favor) in [His] kindness and goodness of heart toward us in Christ Jesus."* (parentheses and brackets are from the AMPC)

That verse is so powerful in the original Greek text! The "coming ages" is "age upon age." The Wuest translation says,

> *"in order that He might exhibit for His own glory* **in the ages that will pile them-**

**selves one upon another in continu-
ous succession,** *the surpassing wealth of His
grace in kindness to us in Christ Jesus."*

I've always thought of eternity as just one big
block of eternity, but it's not going to be that way.
It's going to be divided into ages that can be
differentiated from each other. There will be
differences. That's the only way it can be a different
age is that there's something different about it. And
these ages are going to pile themselves *"one upon
another in continuous succession."*

We don't know what the changes are going to
be or what is in the future, but we do know that we
are going to be the glorious ones—the Church—the
only people who lived in this world at this time who
faced satan and sin in this curse-filled earth, and by
faith we bowed our knees to Jesus and said, "Jesus,
I receive you as my Savior and call you my Lord!"
We are the redeemed ones! There will never again in
any future age be redeemed ones like us because
Jesus isn't going to die again! He'll never die again!
That's been done once and for all eternity!
Hallelujah! This is the chance of eternity that we are
in. We got in on it! We got in on this opportunity to
call on His Name and believe in Him to be saved
and to overcome the world through faith.
Hallelujah! Praise God!

And in the coming *"ages that will pile themselves one upon another in continuous succession,"* He wants to *"show* [us] *the incomparable riches of his grace, expressed in his kindness to us in Christ Jesus."*

Verse 7 says that He might *"show…"* The word "show" literally means "to put on a show and a demonstration." It's like putting on a fireworks show. In the Greek, the word "show" means "to show, demonstrate, prove; to manifest, display, put forth."[11]

God is going to put on a big show and demonstration for us throughout age after age! I think He'll say things like, "Do you like that one? Well, here's another show! Do you like that one? Here's another show. Do you like that one? Here's another show!"

Through age after age, He's going to continue putting on show after show after show of the incomparable riches of His grace (gifts) expressed in His kindness to us, and we're going to be saying, "Wow, God! That was awesome!" He'll say, "Oh, you like that? Here's another one." And we'll say again, "Wow, God, that was awesome!" We're going to be "Wow-ing" all the way through the ages and ages to come as He puts on show after show after show demonstrating His love for us! Glory to God!

Nothing Can Separate Us from the Love of God

God's Word says that nothing can separate us from the love of God! Romans 8:35, 37–39 say:

> [35] *"Who shall separate us from the love of Christ? Shall trouble or hardship or persecution or famine or nakedness or danger or sword?*
>
> [37] *No, in all these things we are more than conquerors through him who loved us.* [38] *For I am convinced that neither death nor life, neither angels nor demons, neither the present nor the future, nor any powers,* [39] *neither height nor depth, nor anything else in all creation [you could say 'neither sin'], will be able to separate us from the love of God that is in Christ Jesus our Lord."*

God's Love Covers and Cleanses Us

I've heard it said sometimes about people coming from really rough, tough, and bad backgrounds that they say, "But you just don't know what I've done. How can you say God loves me? How can you say God can forgive me? You don't know what I've done." Well then, you don't know the power of His blood, and you don't know the power of His love! It doesn't matter what you've done! Jesus died for your sins and paid the full penalty for you! The power of His blood has covered it, cleansed it, and washed it away!

First Peter 4:8 says,

"...love covers over a multitude of sins."

He doesn't even see sin after you are washed in His blood. His blood covers and cleanses you. He doesn't see the past; He doesn't see the sin you committed.

When you receive the blood of Jesus to forgive you and cleanse you, nothing is left of your past—not one thing that you ever did in sin remains. It's all gone! A tidal wave of the blood of Jesus washed it away, and it's gone forever because of the power of His love! And the Bible says that He throws it into the sea (Micah 7:19)—a sea of forgetfulness. He doesn't remember or recall it. In Jeremiah 31:34 and again in Hebrews 8:12 He said,

"For I will forgive their wickedness and will remember their sins no more."

And in Hebrews 10:17 He said,

"Their sins and lawless acts I will remember no more."

Because He *is* Love, He doesn't *want* to see or remember your sin. Why would He want to? He doesn't like it any more than you do. He says, "I don't want to see that. It's under the blood. Don't tell me about it. It's gone. Don't even remind me of it. Just wash in the blood and you're clean." Amen! Praise God!

After you have asked for His forgiveness, if you say, "But God, you know what I did," He says, "No, I don't know." Why? Because He already forgot it, and you need to forget it too! The old has gone, and the new has come. Now you are a new man or a new woman in Christ Jesus, as it says in 2 Corinthians 5:17 (NKJV),

> *"Therefore, if anyone is in Christ, he is a new creation; old things have passed away; behold, all things have become new."*

And 2 Corinthians 5:21 says,

> *"God made him who had no sin to be sin for us, so that in him we might become the righteousness of God."*

When we are born again[7], He gives us a garment of salvation and a robe of righteousness, as He says in Isaiah 61:10,

> *"I delight greatly in the LORD; my soul rejoices in my God. For he has clothed me with garments of salvation and arrayed me in a robe of his righteousness."*

The robe of righteousness is not our righteousness because our righteousness is like filthy rags (Isaiah 64:6). It's His righteousness.

How perfect is Jesus? Very, very, very, very, very, very perfect! And it's His righteousness—His robe of righteousness—that He puts on you. So all you do is walk around remembering, "I'm in Jesus' righteousness. I'm wearing His righteousness. This robe of righteousness is perfect and spotless, and nothing I do will make it dirty because it's His righteousness, and He makes it perfect."

Anytime we make a mistake and sin, all we have to do is say, "Lord, please forgive me and wash me in your blood." 1 John 1:9 says,

> *"If we confess our sins, he is faithful and just and will forgive us our sins and purify us from all unrighteousness."*

When you mess up, quickly take a bath in the blood of Jesus! Dip in His blood like Elisha told Naaman to dip in the river to cleanse him from leprosy (2 Kings 5:1–14). Leprosy in the Bible is a picture of sin, so just like Naaman dipped in the river and was cleansed of leprosy, so you dip in the blood of Jesus, and you will come up whiter than snow (1 John 1:7; Isaiah 1:18; Revelation 7:13–14; Revelation 19:8,14)! Then you are clean again! Your robe is beautiful, and it will never be spotted! Hallelujah!

This is something that we have to practice thinking and remembering because the devil is always giving us that battle of the mind I was talking about and telling us, *"You're no good. You messed up again. You did it again. You're lousy."* He goes on and on and on and beats us up mentally and emotionally. You have to turn on him and say, "Shut up, devil! I'm washed in the blood of Jesus, and the blood of Jesus makes me clean!"

I find also that I like to sing about the blood of Jesus. It helps me get that cleansing flow through my whole spirit and soul and get the condemnation off of me. So I like to sing "Oh the blood of Jesus, oh the blood of Jesus…." And when I start singing it, I feel a cleansing wash over me, and I know the uncleanness is all gone. There's nothing left of it— not one spot, not one piece of dirt of my humanity remains, but what's left is His robe of righteousness. Hallelujah! We wear His robe of righteousness all the time because His love covers over a multitude of sins!

God Has Proven His Love

God has proven His love, so don't ever question it again. Some people say, "God, just show me that you love me!" He already has! Just look at everything He's already done and everything He has already given! Think of Jesus with His arms spread on the cross!

God's great desire to give to mankind is beyond man's comprehension, and although He has demonstrated it throughout history—He has always been faithful to His people to deliver them and bless them—people have blamed God for their problems and hardships when their own ignorance, sin, and rebellion caused it. God has been falsely accused as the One causing sickness, disease, pain, hunger, and death. God has been lied about more than any other person on earth, but He has never done anything but good and shown love to everyone!

Chapter Four

⚜️

Developing a Constant Awareness
of God's Love

As I said previously, *many Christians don't have a true and deep sense and awareness of His love,* which allows fear and doubt to creep in. That's something we have to work on continually because our natural feelings would say otherwise.

So how do we develop that sense and awareness? By meditating on the scriptures every day that we've already talked about (read this book over and over!), and also by the Holy Spirit.

The Holy Spirit Tells Me So

The Lord has helped me work on developing that sense and awareness of His love for me. One time, the song "Jesus Loves Me" was going through my mind: "Jesus loves me this I know for the Bible tells me so." But as I sang it, I thought, *"it's not just the Bible that says so."* So I changed it to my own words, "the Holy Spirit tells me so" because the Holy Spirit is the one who bears witness with our spirit and reveals God to us (John 14:17,20,26; John 16:13–15). And scripture says that He bears witness with our spirit that we are God's children (Romans 8:16).

The Holy Spirit is the one who takes the written Word of God and reveals it to us—makes it revelation knowledge to us. Many people read the Bible and get nothing out of it because it contains secrets that are hidden. The Bible calls it "mysteries that are hidden." First Corinthians 2:7 says,

> *"we speak of* **God's secret wisdom, a wisdom that has been hidden** *and that God destined for our glory before time began."*

The King James Version says,

> *"But we speak the wisdom of God in a* **mystery,** *even the* **hidden wisdom,** *which God ordained before the world unto our glory."*

Second Corinthians 3:14 says,

> *"But their minds were made dull, for to this day the same veil remains when the old covenant* [we could say 'the Bible'] *is read. It has not been removed, because only in Christ is it taken away."*

It is the Holy Spirit who removes the veil and reveals the mysteries in the Bible. First Corinthians 2:9–10 say,

> *"However, as it is written: 'No eye has seen, no ear has heard, no mind has conceived what God has prepared for those who love him'*— **but God has revealed it to us by his Spirit.** *The Spirit searches all things, even the deep things of God."*

So it's not just the Bible that tells me God loves me because that can still be an unrevealed truth—truth without revelation. We know it, but we don't understand or comprehend it. It's a mystery. I've heard "God loves me" all my life, but when the Holy Spirit speaks it to me, it is alive—it is revealed knowledge. When the Holy Spirit says to me, "God loves me," there is a deeper sense and awareness of that love.

So I changed the words of the chorus from "the Bible tells me so" to "the Spirit tells me so." "Jesus loves me this I know for the Spirit tells me so." And the Holy Spirit is bearing witness to it in my heart.

Then I changed the words at the end—"Little ones to Him belong, *I am His and He is mine.*" Singing it that way makes it real to me—***I am His and He is mine***. It creates a bonding in my heart with Him. It creates even a sense of intimate love with Him. This brings more life, light, and personalization to what we know and what we've heard—that God loves us!

The One Jesus Loves

The Apostle John changed his name to "the disciple whom Jesus loved" (John 13:23; 19:26; 20:2). You'll notice when you read his gospel that he doesn't call himself by his name but only as "the disciple whom Jesus loved." You need to change your name also to "the disciple whom Jesus loves." This will also help you identify yourself as the one God loves. You have to make it your own revelation. Say this: "I'm the one Jesus loves. I'm the one Jesus loves. I am His beloved!" Amen! Hallelujah!

The Lord showed me Deuteronomy 33:12 one time as I was reading the Bible, which says,

"About Benjamin he said: "Let the beloved of the LORD rest secure in him, for he shields him all day long, and the one the LORD loves rests between his shoulders."

As I read it, God prompted me to put my name in it. So I said, *"About* [Cherri] *he said: "Let the beloved of the LORD rest secure in him, for he shields* [her] *all day long, and the one the LORD loves* [Cherri] *rests between his shoulders.""*

Now you say, "I am the one the Lord loves. *'Let the beloved of the Lord rest secure in him'*—that's me. *I* am the beloved of the Lord resting securely in Him. He shields *me* all day long. *I* am the one the Lord loves resting between His shoulders." Say it out loud, and let the revelation of being the beloved of the Lord grow in you!

Then remember and personalize other scriptures like Song of Solomon 2:4 (NAS),

"He has brought me to his banquet hall, And his banner over me is love."

Also, Song of Solomon 7:10,

"I belong to my beloved, and his desire is for me."

I belong to Jesus, and His desire is for me!

Believe in His Love!

We *must* believe and not doubt. Your part is to believe it. Your part is to have faith—believe He *does* love you!

First John 4:16 (NKJV) says,

> *"And we have known and **believed** the love that God has for us."*

Believe His love for you! Believe "I am the one the Lord loves. I am the beloved of the Lord. He has called me and chosen me, and He has poured out His gifts and His love on me. I receive it, and I believe it, in Jesus' name!" Hallelujah!

There Is No Fear in Love

Now, as we make a complete circle back to where we started, the stronger the revelation of God's love for you grows in you, the more it will push out all the fear and doubt. Doubts and anxiety come from fear. Worry is fear. And First John 4:18 (KJV) says,

"There is no fear in love; but perfect love casteth out fear: because fear hath torment. He that feareth is not made perfect in love."

He who doubts is not made perfect in love. He who worries is not made perfect in love—that is, in a revelation of God's love. When you know God loves you, it takes away your questions about His will: "Do you want me to prosper? Do you want me to be healed? Do you want me to have a good car? Do you want me to have a good home? Do you want me to have a good marriage? Do you want me to have a good job?" The answer is yes, yes, yes! He loves you! He loves you! He loves you! He wants you to have everything good because He loves you. Everything good in this world is made for you to enjoy because He loves you!

So when you find yourself worrying or doubting, then remember to build your faith in God's love! Focus on His love for you. Say again, "I am the Lord's beloved. He delights in me. He has chosen me. He has called me. He dances and sings over me. He thinks of me continually! He lavishes His gifts on me! He supplies my needs abundantly!" Hallelujah! Amen!

To Know Him Is to Know His Love

First John 4:8 says,

"Whoever does not love does not know God,
because God is love."

God *is* love. **So if you don't know His love, you don't know Him.**

The devil has made people feel unworthy and unloved, and he has painted a picture of a harsh and stingy God—a God who holds everything against you. But it's not true. And if you think that way about God—if you think He's holding back on you—then you don't know Him.

Without a revelation of the love of God, you'll never have close fellowship and communion with Him. There will always be an unwarranted fear, condemnation, guilt, and sometimes even offense against God if you don't know that He loves you. **If you don't know His love, you really don't know Him because He *is* love!** To know *Him* is to know *His love!*

As you fellowship with God in reading the Bible, meditating on these scriptures, and in prayer, you will begin to realize the greatness of His love as it radiates from Him.

Think of the pulsing light and heat that come from the sun: "Whoosh! Whoosh! Whoosh!" Think of each one of those pulses as God's love sweeping over you: "Whoa! I just got whacked by some love! Whoa, I just got whacked by some more love! Wow! The love of God is just about knocking me over! Wow, I'm getting blasted by the love of God as it radiates from Him and sweeps over me!" Hallelujah!

Experience the Fullness of His Love

Paul's prayer for you is also my prayer for you, and it's our prayer—Ephesians 3:17–19:

> *"17so that Christ may dwell in your hearts through faith. And I pray that you, being rooted and established in love, 18 may have power, together with all the saints, to grasp how wide and long and high and deep is the love of Christ, 19 and to* **know** *this love that surpasses knowledge—that you may be filled to the measure of all the fullness of God."*

I pray that as Christ dwells in your heart through faith, you may *"grasp how wide and long and high and deep"* God's love is for you! And that you may also be rooted and established in that love!

The word *"know"* in verse 19 means "to experience in fullness." *"...to **know** this love that surpasses knowledge"* means it's not just head knowledge. It's a full ***experience*** of His love.

"...that you may be filled to the measure of all the fullness of God" means that as you know His love by experience and in fullness, it enables you to be filled to the measure of all the fullness of God—all that God has for you—all of His immeasurable gifts and blessings that He wants to bestow on you.

He is rejoicing over you! He's singing and dancing over you! He has created all of heaven and earth for you! Everything in the earth is for you to enjoy, and God says, "Here take it. I want to give it to you!" Glory, glory! Hallelujah!

The closer you walk with God, the more He is able to manifest His love to you—showing and demonstrating His love to you and pouring out His gifts on you—because you walk with Him like Adam, Abraham, Moses, and David. You ***believe*** in His love. You fellowship with Him. *You* are His friend. *You* are His beloved. *You* are His, and He is yours! Then He's able to do more and more for you!

Say it once again, "Thank you, Jesus, for Your love! Thank you, Father, for Your love! I believe in

Your love for me! Thank you for Your immeasurable, eternal love that You will continue to show in the ages to come, and even now You are giving and pouring out every spiritual and physical gift on me. Thank you, Father! I believe it, and I receive it! Amen!"

❦

Prayer for Salvation

Romans 10:9–11 say, *"if you confess with your mouth, 'Jesus is Lord,' and believe in your heart that God raised him from the dead, you will be saved. [10] For it is with your heart that you believe and are justified, and it is with your mouth that you confess and are saved. [11] As the Scripture says, 'Anyone who trusts in him will never be put to shame.'"*

1 John 1:9 says, *"If we confess our sins, he is faithful and just and will forgive us our sins and purify us from all unrighteousness."*

If you have never asked Jesus to be the Lord of your life, you can pray this prayer:

"Dear Lord Jesus, I know I am a sinner. Please forgive me of my sins and come into my heart and life. You said in Romans 10:9, "If you confess with your mouth, 'Jesus is Lord,' and believe in your heart that God raised him from the dead, you will be saved." So I confess that You, Jesus, are my Lord and Savior, and I believe in my heart that You are the Son of God, You died on the cross for my sins, and God raised You from the dead. Now I give You my life. Please teach me Your ways and help me to serve You all of my life. Thank you for saving me and cleansing me of sin, and making me your child. I give You praise, in Jesus' Name, Amen!"

Notes:

[1] https://www.mcleanbible.org/sites/default/files/ Multiply-Resources/Chap3/ GreekWordsforLoveWS_Chapter3.pdf

[2] Strong, James. *Strong's Exhaustive Concordance of the Bible*. Abingdon Press, 1890.
5387 (Greek dictionary)

[3] Strong's *5360, 5368*

[4] Wuest, Kenneth. *Wuest's Word Studies in the Greek New Testament*. Grand Rapids, Michigan: Wm. B. Eerdmans Publishing Co., 1975. Vol. III Bypaths, pp. 111-113.

[5] Strong's *25*

[6] For more information and study on God's purpose for mankind, read my book *The Story of God's Glorious Plan For Man*.

[7] Born again: John 3:3–6 (NKJV) say,

> [3] *"Jesus answered and said to him, 'Most assuredly, I say to you, unless one is born again, he cannot see the kingdom of God.'* [4] *Nicodemus said to Him, 'How can a man be born when he is old? Can he enter a second time into his mother's womb and be born?'* [5] *Jesus answered,*

'Most assuredly, I say to you, unless one is born of water and the Spirit, he cannot enter the kingdom of God. [6] That which is born of the flesh is flesh, and that which is born of the Spirit is spirit.'"

Also, 1 Peter 1:21,23 say,

"Through him you believe in God, who raised him from the dead and glorified him, and so your faith and hope are in God. [23] For you have been born again, not of perishable seed, but of imperishable, through the living and enduring word of God."

Being born again means your spirit is made new (you are a new creation on the inside—2 Corinthians 5:17) when you believe in and receive Jesus Christ as your personal Savior, and you are born into God's family becoming one of His children. See the prayer for salvation to be born again!

[8] Livingston, Jay, and Evans, Raymond. "Tammy" Performed by the Ames Brothers. Copyright © Jay Livingston Music, 1957.

[2] Strong's *4053*

[10] Strong's *2983*

[11] Strong's *1731*

MORE BOOKS BY CHERRI CAMPBELL

Adventures with Jesus—A Journal of My World Missionary Travels

The Story of God's Glorious Plan for Man

The Baptism in the Holy Spirit & The Benefits of Speaking in Tongues

Go to victoriousfaith.co

About the Author

By jumbo jet and small propeller plane, by ship, small boat, ferry and train, by truck, bus, jeepney, auto rickshaw, automobile, motorcycle, tricycle, and by foot, **Cherri Campbell** has been a traveling missionary in over twenty nations, teaching the Word of God and preaching in Bible schools, ministers' conferences, churches, youth conferences, and women's conferences. She is the author of a one-year Bible school curriculum called *Foundations of Victorious Living*, which has been adopted by several Bible schools. She has lived in the bush in Vanuatu, the Solomon Islands, Papua New Guinea, and the Federated States of Micronesia. She has preached and taught the Word of God in the underground church in Asia, traveled by train preaching across India, taught in conferences in the Himalayas, and preached in Bible schools, churches, and conferences in Southeast Asia, East Africa, and West Africa.

Cherri now lives in Colorado, and in 2013, she began a daily half-hour radio broadcast called *Victorious Faith*, which is also available on her website, *victoriousfaith.co*, and YouTube channel. Her simple yet in-depth teaching style has helped many Christians around the world, including pastors, gain a deeper understanding and practical application of the Word of God to receive healings, supernatural provision, victories, and breakthroughs in their own lives.

Cherri's calling is to train and equip the Body of Christ to live and operate *victoriously* in the Kingdom of God, maturing the saints to *be* a glorious and triumphant Church and to *do* the works of Jesus Christ.